LIKE A YETI CATCHING MARMOTS

Like a Yeti Catching Marmots

A LITTLE TREASURY OF TIBETAN PROVERBS

Pema Tsewang, Shastri

WITH **JOSH BARTOK**

WISDOM PUBLICATIONS • BOSTON

Wisdom Publications
199 Elm Street
Somerville MA 02144 USA
www.wisdompubs.org

Library of Congress Cataloging-in-Publication Data
Padma-tshe-dban, Sastri.
 Like a yeti catching marmots : a little treasury of Tibetan proverbs / Pema Tsewang Shastri.
   p. cm.
 Proverbs in Tibetan and English, with pref. and explanations in English.
 ISBN 1-61429-000-8 (pbk. : alk. paper)
 1. Proverbs, Tibetan—Translations into English. I. Title.
 PN6519.T55P33 2011
 398.9'9541—dc23
                          2011028941

ISBN 9781614290001
eBook ISBN 9781614290155

16 15 14 13 12
5 4 3 2 1

Cover design by Phil Pascuzzo. Interior design by Gopa&Ted2. Set in Cronos Pro 10.5/14.7.

Wisdom Publications' books are printed on acid-free paper and meet the guidelines for permanence and durability of the Production Guidelines for Book Longevity of the Council on Library Resources.

Printed in the United States of America.

This book was produced with environmental mindfulness. We have elected to print this title on 30% PCW recycled paper. As a result, we have saved the following resources: 10 trees, 3 million BTUs of energy, 962 lbs. of greenhouse gases, 4,336 gallons of water, and 275 lbs. of solid waste. For more information, please visit our website, www.wisdompubs.org. This paper is also FSC® certified. For more information, please visit www.fscus.org.

*This book is dedicated
to the long life of the
Tibetan culture.*

Preface

It's said that nothing defines a culture as distinctly as its language—and the element of language that best encapsulates a society's values and beliefs is its proverbs.

The importance of proverbs in the social interaction of Tibetans is best expressed by one such proverb that says: "Honey is sweet to the mouth; proverb is music to the ear." Many of these sayings, naturally glued to the tongues of many Tibetans, are terse and telling, poetic and pithy, and filled with wit and wisdom. These proverbs also reflect the culture of the Tibetan people, who live in *Gang Jong*, "the Land of Snows," on the highest plateau of the world, and possess a distinctive language, culture, history, and way of life.

There is no doubt that the Tibetan proverbs originated with and developed alongside Tibetan civilization. The earliest written record of Tibetan proverbs can be traced to an ancient manuscript discovered in the Dunhuang caves, which contain scrolls from as long ago as the fourth century c.e. One Tibetan proverb on the scrolls there is this: "Don't break a grateful man's heart; don't break the back of a divine horse."

Many of the proverbs carry two meanings; one literal and the other metaphorical. For instance, "Going up with the steps of a louse, going down with the jump of a musk deer" literally means the pace will be slow while climbing up a mountain and the pace will be much quicker while walking down—but it also refers to the difficulty with which one builds spiritual merit and the comparative ease with which it can be wiped away. Structurally, some Tibetan proverbs are quite poetic and beautifully rhymed, some use simile, and others use personification, and some, like "White is easily blackened; long is easily broken," use double analogy for powerful emphasis.

Until recently many aspects of Tibetan folk literature, though very popular, remained oral or unwritten as the majority of the Tibetan population was illiterate or uneducated—and thus many Tibetan proverbs were preserved only in the minds and stories of Tibetan elders. Nonetheless, it wouldn't be an exaggeration to note that Tibet has actually produced the largest amount of literature, per capita, of any country in the world!

Tibetans have always prized a ready and comprehensive knowledge of proverbs so much that a man possessing such knowledge would be hired by others in his home town as legal representation in courtroom battles. Inside these ancient courts, the case was often won by the representative with the highest powers of persuasion—demonstrated through the skillful deployment of the appropriate proverbs.

My late mother, Dawa, was a treasure trove of Tibetan proverbs—and a wonderful storyteller as well. In our daily conversations she used one proverb after another to make a point or bring home some meaning or lesson, often after she had told me part of the great Tibetan epic tale about King Gesar. I learned many, many proverbs this way. Then, in 1994, I started actively collecting the Tibetan proverbs, noting each down whenever I read or heard one.

Except for a few, I have tried to select those Tibetan proverbs that are not only used in all the three provinces of Tibet but also in the Himalayan regions like Nepal, Bhutan, Sikkim, Spiti, Zanskar, and Ladakh—while at the same time picking the ones likely to resonate in some universal way. When the proverb is more or less self-explanatory, I've let it stand on its own; for other proverbs, I've offered a brief gloss of the meaning or a comment, and in some cases—to point to certain universal themes—I've offered a parallel English-language saying. And

ix

in a number of cases, I've taken minor liberties with the English translation to improve readability.

My purpose in presenting this book is twofold: to introduce the wonderful folk wisdom of Tibet to non-Tibetans, and also to encourage and inspire younger Tibetans to acquaint themselves with this unique Tibetan art of expression.

In the process of working on this small book I would like to thank my daughter, Tenzin Dickyi, and my friend Laura Zimmerman for reading the manuscript and helping correct the English renderings of the proverbs.

I'm also grateful to Josh Bartok, senior editor at Wisdom Publications, for his development of the English explanations, and for his meticulous editing. And many thanks to Tim McNeill and Wisdom Publications for bringing out this book.

Pema Tsewang, Shastri

ཇིད་མོས་འཕྱི་བ་བཟུང་བ།

Like a Yeti catching marmots.

The Yeti, or Dremo *in Tibetan, is a dim-witted mythical beast said to feed only on marmots. It sees a marmot, grabs the hapless creature, and then sits on it—saving the delicious morsel for later. And then the Yeti sees another marmot and leaps up to snatch it— while the first marmot makes a quick break for freedom. An image of bumbling, foolish effort— and the pitfalls of greed.*

ཁ་ལ་མངར་མོ་སྦྲང་རྩི་ཡིན། རྣ་ལ་སྙན་པོ་གཏམ་དཔེ་ཡིན།

Honey is sweet to the mouth;
proverb is music to the ear.

དཀའ་བའི་བྲག་ལ་མ་བྱག་ན། བདེ་བའི་སྤང་ལ་སྐྱེ་ནས་མི་ཐུབ།

**You can't get to the meadow of happiness
without climbing the cliff of hardship.**

*Working through the difficulties in our lives is
the only path to contentment.*

དཀའ་ལས་སྐུ་བས་བརྒྱབས། ལོངས་སྤྱོད་ཞ་རུས་བཏང་།

**It is the spatula that worked hard
but it is the ladle that enjoyed the porridge.**

Tibetans make a delicious porridge made from barley, called thugpa.
*When being cooked, this porridge must be stirred continuously with a
spatula. And then, when it's finally ready, the spatula is put aside
and a ladle dips in and serves us the food—
and the spatula's hard work is forgotten!*

དཀར་པོ་ནག་སླ། རིང་པོ་ཆག་སླ།

White is easily blackened; long is easily broken.

Akin to "The bigger they are, the harder they fall."

དཀར་ཡོལ་ཆག་ཀྱང་། རི་མོ་བློ་ངས་ཡིན།

Even though the cup was broken, the pattern lingers in the mind.

This proverb points to the way people and deeds, for instance, live on through their impact on others even after passing away.

འདམ་རྫབ་ནང་དུ་རྟ་ཕོའི་ཤེད་ཤུགས་རྟོགས།

The strength of a horse is known in the marsh.

When we're in a difficult situation, we see who our true friends are—
"A friend in need is a friend indeed."

ཀྱང་པ་རྒྱ་ལ་མ་རེག་པར། ཉ་མོ་ལག་པས་འཛིན་ཐབས་མེད།།

**There is no way to catch a fish by hand
without getting one's feet wet.**

"You can't make an omelet without breaking some eggs."

ཀུན་མ་རང་ལ་བཞག །སྒོ་ལྕགས་ཕྱི་ལ་བརྒྱབས།

Locking the door from outside and leaving the thief inside.

"Leaving the fox to stand guard over the henhouse."

ཀང་གཅིག་གི་སྐུས་མ། ལག་གཅིག་གི་རྫོག་པ།

**Knitting with one needle,
clapping with one hand.**

*This proverb is used akin to two different English proverbs:
"Not playing with a full deck" and also "It takes two to tango."*

སྐྱུང་གས་སྐྱུང་ཀར་ཕུ་རེས་མ་བྱེད། མཆུ་ཏོ་དམར་པོ་འད་འད་རེད།།

**A blackbird shouldn't mock another blackbird,
for both have red beaks.**

*This proverb also evokes two English proverbs:
"That's the pot calling the kettle black"
and
"Those who live in glass houses shouldn't throw stones."*

སྐྱགས་པས་སྐྱང་མདོག་བྱས་པ། མཚོན་གསལ་གནན་ལས་དོད་པ།།

When a fool pretends to be clever,
he looks all the more foolish.

སྔད་གྲགས་སེང་གི་ཆེ་ཡང་། ཕན་ཐོགས་སྐྱི་ཁྱི་ཆེ།

Though the lion is more famous,
the dog is more useful.

The Snow Lion, a celestial creature of luminous white fur and a turquoise mane, is the ubiquitous symbol of the Tibetan people. It symbolizes, among other things, fearlessness and unconditional cheerfulness; it appears on Tibet's flag and in countless other places as well. But since it's a mythic being, no one has ever seen one! The tiny Lhasa Apso dog on the other hand—bred for centuries to resemble a miniature Snow Lion—makes an excellent household sentry. Thus, though much less famous, the dog is more useful. It's the common people and everyday things that make the real difference in our lives, not the celebrities.

ཁྱི་ལ་སེང་གེའི་མིང་བཏགས།

Giving a lion's name to a dog.

"Putting lipstick on pig"—no matter how much you dress it up,
it's still a pig; no matter what you call the dog, it's not a lion.

སྐུ་ལུས་གཅིག་ལ་བརྒྱད་པ་བརྒྱ། ཉི་མ་གཅིག་ལ་འོད་ཟེར་འབུམ།

**A single body with a hundred manifestations,
a single sun with a hundred thousand rays.**

*As the sun emits myriad rays to sustain innumerable lives on earth,
so too does a bodhisattva—a transcendent being whose existence
is dedicated to the service of others—manifest in
countless forms to benefit sentient beings.
An image of selfless generosity.*

སྐེ་བཅད་ནས་འོག་མར་བྱུལ་བྱུལ།

Caressing the chin after cutting the throat.

An insincere or cynically inadequate gesture of apology or restitution.

སྐེ་འཕྱིར་ནས་ཞགས་པ་བཞེད་པ་དང་། རྫ་འཕྱིར་ནས་རྡོ་བོ་བ།

**Inviting the lasso by sticking out one's neck,
inviting stones by bringing out the earthen-pot.**

Asking for trouble—
"The nail that sticks up is the one that is hammered down."

སྐྱ་ཁ་ལ་འཇམ་པ་དང་། ཐང་ཤིང་ལ་མཛེས་པ།།

Comfortable for the magpie
and beautiful for the pine tree.

*Used to describe a win-win situation: The magpie rests comfortably
on the branch of the tree, and the tree looks all the
more beautiful adorned by the bird.*

སྐྱིད་ཀྱི་རྟ་པོ་མཉམ་བཞོན། སྡུག་གི་ཁུར་པོ་མཉམ་འཁུར།

**Ride the horse of happiness together;
bear the load of suffering together.**

*An expression of a couple who together meet all that life brings,
akin to the traditional wedding vow phrase,
"for richer and for poorer."*

སྐྱིད་པོ་རང་གིས་མ་བྱས་ན། སྡུག་པོ་མི་ཡིས་གཏོང་ངེན་ཡོད།

**If you don't make yourself happy,
then others will surely make you suffer.**

*Not taking responsibility for your own happiness
is the surest path to unhappiness.*

སྐྱིད་ནི་མ་གཉིས་ལ་འཆར་དུས་དང་། སྡུག་སྨུན་པ་གཉིས་ལ་ཤེལ་དུས་མེད།།

**Happiness and sunshine have no fixed time for occurring;
suffering and darkness have no fixed time for disappearing.**

*Joys surely come and sorrows surely pass—
but not according to any schedule.*

སྐྱུར་མོ་ཞིག་དང་མ་འཕྲད་ན། མངར་མོ་ཐམས་ཅད་ཅང་ཅང་རེད།

If one has not met with sourness,
every sweet thing would taste dull.

Our sorrows enable us to better appreciate life's sweetness;
our enemies help us to appreciate our friends.

སེམས་པོ་རབ་གཅིག་གི་ཁོག་པ་ལ། ཁོང་ཐང་དཀར་ཁྱིང་བསྐོར་རྒྱག་ས་ཡོད།
སེམས་པོ་འབྲིང་གཅིག་གི་ཁོག་པ་ལ། མདའ་གྱི་མདུང་གསུམ་ཕོངས་ས་ཡོད།
སེམས་པོ་ཐ་ཞིག་གི་ཁོག་པ་ལ། རྒྱ་ཁབ་ཕུ་མོ་ཐར་ས་མེད།

**In the heart of an inferior man, there is not space
even for a needle.
In the heart of a mediocre man, there is space for a spear.
In the heart of a superior man, there is space enough
for an eagle to soar.**

*The heart of an inferior person is closed and constricted and he cares
only for himself; a middling person's heart is a little more
accommodative; but a superior person's heart is vast
and spacious, open to the entire world.*

LIKE A YETI CATCHING MARMOTS

སྐྱེ་དུས་ཆགས་པ་མི་དྲན། ཆགས་དུས་སྐྱེ་བ་མི་དྲན།

Caught in the pain of giving birth,
one does not remember the desire that led to it;
caught up in desire,
one does not imagine the pain of labor to come.

ཁ་ནོར་ན་ཕྱིར་འཐེན་བྱེད་ཐབས་མེད། ལམ་ནོར་ན་ཕྱིར་ལོག་བྱེད་ས་ཡོད།

**One cannot withdraw what is spoken from one's mouth,
but one can always return back from a mistaken path.**

You can't unsay what is said, but it's always possible to make amends.

ཁ་འོ་མ་ཁོག་ཚེར་མ།

Milky mouth, thorny heart.

A person's words may be soft and smooth—
and a deceitful cover of the ill-will within.

ཁ་བཤད་ཆུ་ཡི་ལྦུ་བ། ལག་ལེན་གསེར་གྱི་ཐིག་པ།

Speech is a water bubble;
implementation is a drop of gold.

It's easy to talk a good game, but really doing it is what matters—
"Walk the walk, don't just talk the talk."

ཁ་གཅིག་ལ་ཁོག་པ་མི་གཅིག སྔས་གཅིག་ལ་རྨི་ལམ་མི་གཅིག།

One mouth, different thoughts;
one pillow, different dreams.

The first part of this proverb refers to the fact that a single person—
"one mouth"—may, according to circumstances and conditions
and audience, express different and even seemingly contradictory
sentiments. The second part refers to the fact that in Tibet,
unlike in the West, pillows are large and long enough to accommodate
multiple heads at once, such as those of a husband and wife,
or of several siblings. But even sharing a pillow thus doesn't mean
they will have the same dreams at night.

ཁ་ནང་གི་རྨ་ཁ་ནང་དུ་གསོ་དགོས།

The wound within the mouth must be healed inside the mouth.

This proverb is used akin to "Don't air your dirty laundry in public"—
settle private matters privately.

ཁ་ཟས་སྤང་ནས་བཟས། རི་ལ་མ་ནགས་སུ་བཏང་།།

**Eating grass from the pasture
but carrying one's dung to the forest.**

*Dung is, of course, excellent fertilizer that could help a pasture grow
lush. This image is one of using resources in one place
but returning the beneficial "fruit" elsewhere.*

ཁམ་བུ་བཟའ་འདོད་མེད་པར། སྐྱུར་ཁ་སྐྱུར་ལ་བཏགས།

While not wanting to eat a peach,
the pretext was put on its sourness.

Though often associated with warm climates, the peach is actually quite
common in Tibet, especially in the provinces of Lhasa and Kongpo,
for instance. This is an image of giving spurious excuses to
justify what you've already decided you want to do.

ཁོང་ཁྲོ་སློང་མཁན་མེད་ན། བཟོད་པ་སུ་ལ་སྒོམ།

**When there is no one to provoke anger,
how shall we practice patience?**

*It's only our seeming adversaries who give us the opportunity to develop
the virtue of patience; if everything always went our way and
everyone always did or said exactly what we'd wish,
we'd have no cause to refine our character and
develop wholesome qualities.*

ཁོང་ཁྲོ་ལྟ་བུའི་སྡུག་བསྔལ་མེད། །བཟོད་པ་ལྟ་བུའི་དཀའ་ཐུབ་མེད།

There is no suffering like anger;
there is no penance like patience.

Anger is it's own punishment,
and patience is its own reward.

ཁོང་ཁྲོ་གཡག་ལ་ཟ། རྟོག་རྒྱག་རྫེལ་ལ་གཞུས།

Angry at the yak but kicking the mule.

An image of displaced anger that erupts in
inappropriate or undeserved places.

ཁོག་ནང་དུ་མེ་འབར་ཡང་། དུ་བ་ཁ་ནས་མ་བཏོན།

**Even though your heart burns,
don't let smoke come out of your mouth.**

*Sometimes it's best to just keep your mouth shut—
no matter how angry or hurt you may feel.*

LIKE A YETI CATCHING MARMOTS

ཁྱོད་ཀྱིས་ལམ་ལ་བསྐྱོད་པ་ལས། ང་ཡིས་ཟམ་པ་བརྒལ་བ་མང་།

I have crossed more bridges than you have walked on the road.

Akin to expressions like "I have more experience in my little finger
than you do in your entire life." It also refers to the
worldly experience gained in travel.

ཁྲིམས་ཀྱིས་བསྐྱམས་ན་བརྒྱ་དང་། ཐག་པས་བསྐྱམས་ན་གཅིག

A law binds hundreds of people;
a rope binds just one.

An image of casting too wide a net; making an onerous law
binding everyone, when just "tying up" the lone
transgressor would be more sensible.

མཁས་པས་ཤེས་ཡོན་ནོར་ལ་བརྩི། སྐྱེན་པས་གསེར་དངུལ་ནོར་ལ་བརྩི།

The foolish think riches are gold and silver;
the wise know that learning is wealth.

མཁས་ཀྱང་དོན་ལ་མ་དཔྱད་ན། ས་འོག་གསེར་གྱི་མདངས་དང་འདྲ།

**Even to a wise man, meaning that is not studied
is like the light of buried gold.**

*Akin to Socrates's statement that
"The unexamined life is not worth living."
Also: even the wise must study and
work to refine their wisdom.*

གང་ལ་དགའ་ན་དེ་ལ་མཁས།

One becomes skilled in what one likes.

གོམ་གཅིག་མ་སྤོས་སྐྱིང་བཞི་མི་འཁོར།
ཆུ་ཐིགས་མ་བསགས་རྒྱ་མཚོ་མི་ཡོང་།

**One cannot reach four corners of the world
unless one makes the first step;
the ocean is not possible without
the collection of water drops.**

*"A journey of a thousand miles begins with a single step"—
and great deeds are accomplished bit by bit.*

གོས་ཆེན་ཐོག་ལ་འཚེམ་དྲུབ། རལ་པའི་ཐོག་ལ་ལྷན་པ།

Embroidery upon brocade,
a patch upon a rip.

A phrase contrasting unnecessary embellishment on something
already beautiful with a simple and necessary fix.

གྱེན་རེ་འཛེགས་ན་ཐུར་རེ་ཡོང་།

Every incline has a decline.

"What goes up must come down."

བློག་མ་ལུས་ལ་རྟ་ཆ་བ་དེ། ཏ་ཐོག་མི་ཡིས་ག་ལ་མཐོང་།

**How can the man on the horse see
the ant struggling for survival?**

*"You can't truly know another's difficulties until you've walked a mile
in his shoes, and you know for yourself where the shoe pinches."
Everyone has difficulties in life, we just don't always see them.*

བློ་གྲོས་པོ་བསྐུ་དུས་དགོད་བཞིན་བསྐུ། ཁྲམ་པས་བསྐུ་དུས་དུ་བཞིན་བསྐུ།

**Some deceive you with a smile;
others deceive you by weeping.**

*Seeming kind, one "friend" may use flattery to manipulate and deceive,
another may weep "crocodile tears," making a grand display of
insincere feeling. Also used to remind us to beware getting
too caught up in others' reactions—or in our own!*

གྲོས་མི་ལ་དྲིས། ཐག་རང་གིས་གཅོད།

**Ask others for suggestions,
make the decision yourself.**

མགོ་སྐྲ་མེད་ལ་རལ་པའི་ཁྲལ།

The bald man having to pay a tax on braids.

An image of bearing a burden but reaping no benefit.

མགོ་རེ་ལ་རེ་ལ་ཐམས་ཅད་དགེ་སློང་དང་། །

ལུས་སེར་སེར་ཐམས་ཅད་བླ་མ་མིན། །

All with shaved heads are not monks;
all with saffron robes are not lamas.

"All that glitters is not gold"—
especially when it comes to people.

འགྲོ་ཉེར་ན་ཆུ་སྟ་བཏོལ་འདྲ་དགོས། སྡོད་ཉེར་ན་རྒྱ་མཚོ་འབྱིལ་འདྲ་དགོས།

**Going forth, be like water bursting out;
staying at rest, be like the calm sea.**

*When you do something, really do it wholeheartedly;
when you cease, really let it go.*

ཚོད་པོ་འཁྲིད་ན་མཐུར་མདའ་རིང་དགོས།
སྡོང་ཁན་གཅོད་ན་སྟ་ཡུ་རིང་དགོས།

**One needs a long rein to lead an untamed horse;
one needs an axe with a long handle to chop
down an ancient tree.**

*To control the strong-willed, sometimes one needs
to take a few steps back and give them more space.*

རྒྱགས་དུས་ཆོས་དྲན། ལྟོགས་དུས་ཀུ་དྲན།

**One thinks of Dharma when the stomach is full;
one thinks of stealing when the stomach is empty.**

*It's easy to think holy thoughts in comfort and privilege,
but doing so in hardship too is the real test.*

སྒོང་ངའི་ནང་གི་སེར་རིལ། ཨ་ཡོད་ནང་གི་ད་ཡོད།

The yolk from the egg, the best among those present.

Tibetans regard the yolk as the "essence" of the egg, and the most tasty part—this image is akin to "the cream of the crop."

སྒོག་པ་ལྐོག་ལ་བཟས་ཀྱང་། སྒོག་དྲི་ངོས་ལ་ཁ་བ།།

**The smell of garlic can be sniffed from afar
even though the garlic was eaten in secrecy.**

You can hide the deed but not the consequences.

སྒྲོན་མེ་འོད་གསལ་ཡང་། རང་གི་ཞབས་རས་མི་མཐོང་།

**Even though the lamp is bright,
it cannot see beneath its own base.**

Even the wisest have their blind spots.

བགད་དེ་བརྒྱ་ཐུབ། ཁྲོས་ཏེ་གཅིག་མི་ཐུབ།

A smile wins a hundred hearts;
a frown not even one.

ངོ་བསྟོད་ཀྱིས་གཉེན་མི་འཕྲོངས། ཚིག་རྩུབ་ཀྱིས་དགྲ་མི་འཕུལ།

Praise alone will not sustain friends;
harsh words cannot vanquish foes.

Akin to "Action speaks louder than words"
or "Fine words butter no parsnips."

ང་ཚིགས་ལ་དཔག་པའི་ཞབས་བྲོ་རྐྱབས།

One must dance according to the beats of the drum.

Akin to both "When in Rome, do as the Romans do" and
"You've got to play the game with the cards you're dealt."

སྔར་དུག་སྦྲུལ་ནག་པོས་སྐྲག་པ་ཅན། དཔེ་གུ་ཁ་ཁྲ་ཡིད་མི་ཆེས།།

Once frightened by a poisonous snake,
now one fears even a striped rope.

An image of overgeneralized anxiety—"Once bitten, twice shy."

གཅན་གཟན་གྱིས་ཀྱང་རང་རྐུད་མི་ཟ།

Even the wild animals do not eat one of their own.

Akin to "There is honor among thieves."

ལྕགས་ཚ་ཐོག་ལ་རྡུངས། ཀོ་བ་རློན་ཐོག་ལ་མཉེད།།

**Hit the iron when it's hot;
cure the leather when it's wet.**

*The first part of this proverb has an almost exact parallel
in English: "Strike while the iron is hot."*

ལྗང་མར་ལྗང་སྐྱོར་མ་ཐུབ་རུང་། ལྗང་རྩ་རྡོ་ཡིས་རྡང་མི་ཉེན།

**Even if you can't build a fence to protect the sapling,
at least avoid stacking stones on its roots.**

Even if you can't help, at least do less harm.

བཏད་པའི་ཤུལ་ལ་བཙུགས་པ་འདྲ་བ།

Stabbed on the same spot where the cut was.

"Rubbing salt in the wound" or reawakening past hurts.

ཆག་སྟོ་བྱུང་ན་འགོ་དང་། སྲུ་གི་བྱུང་ན་མཐའ།

Disaster strikes at the top; famine strikes at the bottom.

Here disaster *refers mainly to the problems thought about
by leaders and people in charge—like, for instance, a precipitous fall
in the exchange rate of a country's currency. Such things are not
generally the concern of the general populace. But such troubles
like famine—when basic resources are themselves very scarce—
are mainly felt by the common person, and a nation's elite
will rarely be the first to go unnourished.*

ཚམས་པར་ཕན་ཡང་། ཡ་མར་གཏོང་།།

That which cures the cold inflames the sinus.

Sometimes the medicine can be as bad as the affliction.
Also akin to "Out of the frying pan, into the fire."

ཚང་ལ་རྒུ་འཇལ། བཟང་ལན་ངན་འཇལ།

Repaying water for wine
and cruelty for kindness.

Images of ingratitude and unequal consideration.

ཆུ་དཀྲོགས་ནས་མར་མི་འབྱིན། རྡོ་གཡམ་བཙིར་ནས་སྣུམ་མི་ལོན།

**You can't make butter by churning water;
you can't get oil by squeezing slate.**

*Some things are just impossible—
"You can't squeeze blood from a stone."*

ཆུ་ལ་རྒྱག་པ་གཞུས་ནས། ཉ་ལ་ཁྱི་ཡང་མེད།

**You can beat the lake with a stick,
but it won't matter to the fish.**

*An image of ineffectual aggression—like "spitting into the wind."
Also an image for angry words or deeds
that roll off someone "like water off a duck's back."*

ཆུ་ཆར་པའི་སྐྱོར་རོ་གས་མ་བྱུང་ཡང་། སད་སེར་བའི་སྐུ་འདྲེན་མ་བྱེད།

Don't call down hail, even if you can't summon rain.

This proverb comes from the belief that certain great yogis can develop supernatural powers—even going so far as to be able to influence the weather! Accordingly, this proverb says that if you can't helpfully summon nourishing rain, you should at least refrain from causing devastating hail.

ཆུ་བོ་ཆུང་ཆུང་འུར་སྒྲ་ཆེ། ཡོན་ཏན་ཆུང་ཆུང་ང་རྒྱལ་ཆེ།

A small stream makes more sound; fools are the ones who brag.

Akin to Plato's statement: "As empty vessels make the loudest sound, so they that have the least wit are the greatest babblers."

ཆུ་འཚོག་པའི་སྣོད་ཡོད་ཀྱང་། གཏམ་འཚོག་པའི་སྣོད་མེད།

**There are vessels that can capture water
but none that can capture words.**

*Water can be caught and contained,
but nothing can stop the spread of gossip.*

གནམ་ལ་རྟོག་རྒྱག་གཞུས་ན། སྣག་ཁུང་རྡོ་ལ་བརྡབ་ཡོང་།

**If you try to kick the sky,
you'll only hit the back of your head on the ground
(when you fall over backward).**

*Images of ineffectuality, especially ineffectual anger—
and also akin to "Spitting into the wind."*

ཆུ་ཆུང་དུས་ཆུ་རགས་ལ་བརྒྱབས་ན། ལུང་ཆུང་རྒྱ་ཡིས་འབྲིར་ཉེན་ཡོད། མེ་ཆུང་དུས་མེ་སྣགས་ལ་བསད་ན། ནགས་སྟུག་པོ་མེ་ཡིས་འཚིག་ཉེན་ཡོད།

If the dike is not built when the water is low,
the valley may be flooded.
If the fire is not extinguished when the ember is tiny,
the thick forests may be lost to fire.

It's essential to take action at the first sign of a problem.
"A stitch in time saves nine."

ཚོག་ཤེས་ལྡན་ན། ནོར་ལ་མང་ཉུང་མེད།

**If one possesses contentment,
less or more wealth makes no difference.**

ཀུན་དང་མཐུན་པ་མི་ཆོས་རྩ་བ་ཡིན།

To live in harmony is the essence of human morality.

*In the Tibetan culture, so deeply influenced for centuries by Buddhism,
morality is not found in the adherence to rules as such, but rather
through living harmoniously with each other and the world.*

ཆོས་མི་ལ་སྟོན་པར། རང་ཉིད་སྒྲིམ་པ་གཅང་དགོས།།

**In order to teach Dharma to others,
one needs to have a pure morality.**

*In Tibetan Buddhism, the most important quality a guru must possess
is a capacity to act unfailingly in keeping with the highest ethical
standards, the moral precepts of Buddhism. Without that,
a teacher is not truly teaching Dharma.*

ཇ་ཚྭ་མེད་དང་གཏམ་འཚོ་མེད།

**Tea without salt,
speech without meaning.**

*Traditionally, the Tibetans add salt to their tea, and to them that
is what makes tea delicious and worth drinking. Tea without salt
is an image of hollow or empty words.*

འཇའ་ཁ་དོག་མཚར་གྱང་སྙིང་པོ་མེད།

**Even though the colors of rainbows are wonderful,
they are essenceless.**

*Superficial attractiveness in itself serves no real function. Also a reminder
that, in the words of the Heart Sutra, "form is emptiness."*

བྱུས་དཔོན་མང་ན་བྱུས་ཉེས་ཤོར།

Too many strategists make the plan fail.

"Too many cooks spoil the broth."

ཕྲོན་ཤིང་སྐམ་པོར་འབྲས་བུའི་རེ་བ་མེད།

You can't expect fruit from a dried plant.

An image of something that just isn't going to happen.

ཉ་བསད་ནས་ཁྱི་ལ་སྦྱིན་པ་བཏང་།

Killing the fish to feed the dog.

Akin to "Robbing Peter to pay Paul."

LIKE A YETI CATCHING MARMOTS

ཨ་མ་ཚོག་བཀོག་ནས། རྐུབ་ཀྱི་སྣན་པ།

Patching one's ass by cutting off one's ear.

An image for something that fixes one problem by causing another,
such as trying to mend a robe by cutting off its sleeve to make a patch.

ཉལ་ཁ་ལ་ཆུ་མ་མང་། ཤི་ཁ་ལ་ཁ་མ་མང་།

**Don't drink too much before sleeping;
don't talk too much before dying.**

*In ancient Tibet there were hardly any indoor toilets and so people had
to get up and go outside into the frigid air to ease themselves in the
middle of night—so drinking too much before bed was a very bad
idea. Similarly, even on your deathbed it's important to be
especially mindful of how you use your speech.*

ཉི་འོད་སྐྱུར་མོས་མི་ཁེབས།

Sunshine cannot be blocked by a hand.

*A truly good deed or manifest wholesome benefit cannot be
besmirched even by lies, rumors, or half-truths.*

གཉིད་མ་ཉལ་གོང་ལ་རྨི་ལམ་བཤད།

Telling the dream before one has slept.

Akin to "counting the chickens before they're hatched."

གཏམ་ལ་རྩ་ངར་མེད་ཀྱང་། མི་སྙིང་དུམ་བུར་གཏུབས།

Even though harsh speech has no sharp edge,
it can cut the human heart to pieces.

རྟ་རྒོད་པོ་ཤོར་ན་འཛིན་ཐབས་ཡོད།
ཚིག་རྒོད་པོ་ཤོར་ན་འཛིན་ཐབས་མེད།

**A wild horse can be caught if it escapes;
a harsh word cannot be caught if it escapes.**

*Be careful with your speech—something said in the heat
of anger cannot be unsaid.*

ཏེ་ནན་ནས་བཅོས་བྱས་པ་དན་ལ་མཛོན།
ཕག་པ་རྡོང་གསོས་བརྒྱབས་པ་བཟང་པོར་མཛོན།

**An old horse, treated for its back sore, considers it as torture;
a pig, well fed for its meat, considers it as kindness.**

*Sometimes what seems like cruelty is kindness
and sometimes what seems like kindness is not.*

སྟག་ལ་མཆོངས་ཆེན་བཅོ་བརྒྱད་ཡོད་ན། ཝ་ལ་འཛུལ་ཁུང་བཅུ་དགུ་ཡོད།

If the tiger has eighteen great leaps,
the fox has nineteen hiding holes.

An image of being well-prepared for all eventualities.

བཙན་པོས་བསྐུལ་པ་གང་ཡང་མེད།

Caution has betrayed no one.

Akin to Shakespeare's "The better part of valor is discretion."

ཕྱག་ཁོག་གཅིག་ལ་ཐུར་བུ་གཉིས། སྲི་ཤུབས་གཅིག་ལ་སྟ་ཐང་གཉིས།།

One pot with two ladles, one sheath with two swords.

*Two ladles get in each other's way; two swords won't fit
in the same sheath. Also, akin to the Biblical saying that
"You can't serve two masters."*

ཐོས་པ་བརྒྱ་ལས། མཐོང་བ་གཅིག་ལྷག

Seeing once is far better than hearing one hundred times.

"A picture is worth a thousand words."

མཐོ་ན་དགའ་སྟེ། དམའ་ན་བརྟན།།

Though it is better to be higher, it is more stable to be lower.

"Uneasy lies the head that wears the crown."

དར་དུས་དགྲ་ཡང་གཉེན། གྱུད་དུས་གཉེན་ཡང་དགྲ

**When prosperous, even enemies become friends;
when poor, even relatives turn into enemies.**

*When things are going well for you it's easy to collect hangers-on,
but when the storm comes you are often abandoned even
by those who should be closest.*

དུག་སྦྲུལ་ཡིན་པའི་རྗེས་ལ། ཕྲ་སྦོམ་གང་ལ་ཁྱད་མེད།

**If the snake is poisonous,
it does not matter whether it is thick or thin.**

Sometimes knowing details is not relevant to the matter at hand.

བདེན་པ་མར་ཡིན་ཡང་མི་བཞུ། རྫུན་མ་ལྕགས་ཡིན་ཡང་མཐིལ་བརྫོལ།

If truth were butter, it wouldn't melt;
if lies were iron, they would still break.

Truth has value, weight, and intrinsic durability,
whereas even the best lie is fragile and worthless.

མདའ་གཅིག་གིས་ཤ་བ་གཉིས་བསད།

Killing two deer with one arrow.

"Killing two birds with one stone."

འདྲིས་ཆེ་ན་སེང་གེ་ཁྱི་ཡིས་རྨུག ཐག་ཉེ་ན་མིག་གིས་རྫི་མ་མི་མཐོང་།།

Too much familiarity makes a dog bite a lion;
too much intimacy makes the eyes overlook eyelashes.

Akin to "Familiarity breeds contempt"—and also a reminder that
we tend to overlook the needs of those closest to us.

འདོད་པས་ངོ་ཚ་བསྐྱོབས།

Desire eclipses decency.

རྡོ་ཆུང་ཡང་རྟ་བཅོག མེ་ཆུང་ཡང་སྤུ་འཚིགས།

**However small a stone may be, it can break a pot;
however small a fire may be, it can singe your hair.**

Small things can still have an impact.

ནད་པ་རྙིང་པོ་ཨེམ་རྗེ་ཡིན།

An old patient is a doctor.

Our experience—especially of hardship—makes us wise
and able to be of service to others.

ནོར་བུ་ལག་ཏུ་ཡོད་དུས་ནོར་ཉམས་མ་ཚོད།

**When the jewel was in hand,
its worth was not recognized.**

"You don't know what you've got 'till it's gone."

ནེ་ཙོ་སྐྲ་བས་གཟེབ་ཏུ་ཚུད། འདབ་ཆགས་ལྷུག་གས་པ་བདེ་བར་རྒྱུ།།

The parrot is caged because it can talk;
other birds move freely because they cannot.

Sometimes it's being too special that gets us into trouble.

ཕུས་མོ་བཙུགས་ནས་གསོན་པ་ལས། དྲང་པོར་ལངས་ནས་ཤི་ན་དགའ།

Better to die on your feet than to live on your knees.

དཔའ་དུས་དཔོན་ལ་ཡ་པོ་བཟུང་། སྐྱར་དུས་ཁྱི་ལ་ཕྱག་འབུལ་ཞུ།

The brave challenge authority;
the cowardly salute even a dog.

སྐྱེ་པའི་ཞིང་ལ་སྣེར་གྱི་ཐོང་གཤོལ་བཙུགས།

To use a personal plow on the public field.

"Dipping your pen in the company ink."

སྡུག་བསྔལ་དུག་ཀྱང་སྨན་དུ་འགྱུར།

**Even poison can be turned into medicine
if one knows how to use it.**

*What's harmful to some in some circumstances can be beneficial to
others in other circumstances. One traditional Tibetan image is that of
a peacock that can eat from a grove of poisonous plants and transform
the plants into beautiful plumage—similarly, through training
the mind we can use our anger and grasping as fuel
for developing kindness and wisdom.*

ཕ་སྤུན་དགྲ་ལ་ལངས་ཀྱང་། དུས་པ་གསེར།

**Even though one's relatives rose up as enemies,
their bones are as dear as gold.**

*We may fight with our relatives all our lives, but it's best
to remember only the good when they've died—and even in life,
amid struggle, the blood connection still remains.*

ཕག་པས་བསྒས་ན། ཕག་ཚང་གཞལ་ཡས་ཁང་།

A pig sees its own sty as a divine abode.

ཕག་པས་གནམ་མཐོང་བ་དུས་གཅིག་ཡིན།

A pig sees the sky only once.

*Images of shortsighted ignorance and complacent contentment
with worldly circumstances at the cost of spiritual
development—the truth and true cost of which only
become clear at the time of death.*

ཕར་སོང་གི་མི་ལ་རྐུར་ཡོང་གི་གཏམ།

**A man who makes a journey has
a story when he returns.**

ཕོ་རབ་གཏམ་གྱིས་བསླུས། ཕོ་འབྲིང་རྒྱུ་ཡིས་བསླུས། ཕོ་ཐ་རས་ཀྱིས་བསླུས།

**A superior man is deceived by speech;
a middling man is deceived by wealth;
a lowly man is deceived by food.**

*It takes a fine argument to deceive a superior man, a middling one
assumes that wealth goes along with righteousness, and a fool will
believe anything if it comes with a moment of satisfaction.*

ཕོ་རབ་ཀྱི་གཏམ་ནི་མཁོ་དུས་བཤད། ཕོ་འབྲིང་གི་གཏམ་ནི་འདྲི་དུས་བཤད། ཕོ་ཐ་མའི་གཏམ་ནི་རྒྱབ་ཏུ་བཤད།

A superior man talks when required;
a middling man talks when asked;
a lowly man talks when the back is turned.

Speech is powerful—but wisdom is often expressed in silence.
The wise use speech when necessary, the middling when
invited, and the lowly gossip wantonly.

ཕོ་རབ་རྩོད་རྒྱུ་སྤྱི་བྱུས། ཕོ་འབྲིང་རྩོད་རྒྱུ་རང་བྱུས། ཕོ་ཐ་རྩོད་རྒྱུ་ཁ་ཕོར།

A superior man argues for communal welfare;
a middling man argues for self-interest;
a lowly man argues for his own bowl.

A wise person looks to the good of all, a middling one only to his
ultimate self-interest, and a lowly person looks no further
than immediate gratification.

ཕོ་རང་ཚོད་ཟིན་ན་རྒྱལ་པོ་དང་། ཟས་ཟ་ཚོད་ཟིན་ན་སྨན་པ་ཡིན།

He who can control himself is a king;
he who can limit his diet is a doctor.

Self-restraint is the highest freedom and the best medicine.

LIKE A YETI CATCHING MARMOTS

བོང་བུ་བཞོན་ནས། བོང་བུ་འཚོལ་བ།

Looking for the donkey while riding on it.

Akin to "He couldn't find the nose on his face."

LIKE A YETI CATCHING MARMOTS

བྱ་མ་འདྲོགས་པར། སྒོ་ང་ལོན་ཐབས།

Snatching the egg without frightening the hen.

An image of effective effort, requiring delicacy and skill.

བློན་པོས་བསྟོད་པ་ལས། མཁས་པས་སྐྱོད་པ་དགའ།

**It is better to be denounced by the wise
than praised by fools.**

*Even the censure of wise people can be put to good use
if we let it alter our unwholesome behavior—
but even praise from fools is unhelpful.*

ཐུན་པོས་ནོར་ན་གཅིག་ནོར། མཁས་པས་ནོར་ན་བརྒྱ་ནོར།

A mistake committed by a fool is one mistake;
a mistake committed by a wise man is hundreds of mistakes.

When teachers or other people in respected roles of leadership make
mistakes, the consequences multiply because so many people
look to them for guidance and example. No one
looks to a fool for such things.

ཤིང་ལས་བྱུས་པའི་སེང་གེ་དེ། འཇིགས་འཇིགས་འདུག་ཡང་སྙིང་པོ་མེད།

A lion made from wood, though impressive, is devoid of essence.

*A "paper tiger"—someone or something that appears
powerful but has nothing behind the appearance.*

དབུལ་པོ་ལ་རྒྱུ་ཡོད་ན། ཕྱུག་པོ་གཉིད་མི་ཁུག

When a poor man possesses wealth the rich man can't sleep.

Akin to Gore Vidal's comment: "It's not enough
that I succeed—others must fail."

སྦལ་པ་རྐ་ཅན་གཅིག་གིས་སྦལ་ཚང་ཕུང་།

One sick frog will destroy a whole colony of frogs.

"One bad apple spoils the barrel."

སྦལ་པ་མཐོང་དུས། ཚང་མོ་སངས་རྒྱས་རེད།

When one sees the toad, the tadpole is a Buddha.

Though not beautiful by any stretch of the imagination,
compared to the ugliness of a full-grown toad,
a tadpole can seem much more appealing—
if only because it's smaller.
Used in circumstances where one might say in English
that someone or something is "the lesser of two evils."

འབྲུག་སྒྲ་ཆེ་ལ་ཆར་ཐག་ཐུང་།

Great thunder and only brief rain.

All talk and little action; all style and little substance.

མ་འགྱུར་ན་བློ་མིན། མ་ཁྲུགས་ན་སེམས་མིན།

An unchanging mind is not a mind;
an unforgiving heart is not a heart.

If you're incapable of changing your mind when necessary, you're a fool.
If you're incapable of forgiveness, you may as well be heartless.

LIKE A YETI CATCHING MARMOTS

མང་པོའི་དཀྱིལ་དུ་ཁ་ལ་བརྟག གཅིག་པུར་སྡོད་དུས་སེམས་ལ་བརྟག

Examine your speech when in public;
examine your mind when alone.

Be careful what you say when around others;
be careful what you think by yourself.

མི་སེམས་གཅིག་ཏུ་བསྒྲིལ་ན། རི་རྒྱལ་ལྷུན་པོ་སྤོ་ཐུབ།

**If all the minds of men were united,
they could move even Mount Meru from its place.**

*According to Buddhist cosmology, Mount Meru (also known as
Mount Sumeru) is a vast mountain in the center of the world—
but even such a great mountain is no match for unity of will.
Also akin to "Many hands make light work."*

མི་ཁོག་མིས་མི་ལྡན། རྡོ་ཁོག་ཆུ་ཡིས་མི་ལྡན།

**The depth of one human heart cannot be
understood by another;
the core of a stone cannot be plumbed by water.**

*An image of the difficulty of ever really
knowing another person's heart.*

མི་ཡུལ་འོད་ཀྱིས་བརྒྱངས། རང་ཡུལ་སྟོང་པར་བཞག།

Illuminating another's country, leaving one's own dark.

Caring about those afar while ignoring those nearest by.

མི་མང་ཁ་ནི་དུག་ཡིན། མི་མང་ལག་པ་གསེར་ཡིན།

The mouths of the many are poison;
the hands of the many are gold.

When a group of people stands idly by caught up in gossip,
much harm is done; but when they join together in common
purpose, much good can be accomplished.

མི་རྒན་པའི་ཁ་ལ་ཉོན། བྱ་གཞོན་པའི་སྒྲོ་ལ་ལྟོས།

Listen to the advice of old people;
look to the feathers of young birds.

Of birds, the young ones have the prettier feathers;
of people, the old ones, because they're more experienced and wiser,
give the better advice.

མེ་དུ་བ་མེད་པར་གཏོང་མི་ཤེས། ཆུ་རླངས་པ་མེད་པར་སྐོལ་མི་ཤེས།

You cannot make a fire without smoke;
you cannot boil water without steam.

མེ་འབར་བའི་སྟེང་དུ་ཤིང་ཤག་པ།

Adding pieces of wood to the burning fire.

Akin to "Adding insult to injury" and also an image of "Fanning the flames" of discord.

མ་བྱ་དང་ཁྭ་ཏ་མི་འགྲོགས། གླང་ཆེན་དང་བ་གླང་མི་སྦྱིབ།

A peacock and a crow are never friends;
an elephant and a cow never mate.

"Oil and water never mix."

ཚན་དན་ཤུག་པའི་ཀ་བ་གཉིས། མདུང་མ་འདེགས་པའི་ནུས་པ་མཚུངས།

**The pillar made of sandalwood and
the pillar made of cypress offer equal support to the beam.**

*Sometimes all that matters is that a thing gets done,
regardless of how or by whom.*

ཙན་དན་གྱི་གུ་གཡོག ་གོས་ཆེན་གྱི་ཕབ་ཕྱིས།

Sandalwood as kindling, brocade as the kitchen mop.

Images of wasted finery—
"Like throwing pearls before swine."

ཙི་ཙི་མ་མས་གྲོས་བྱས་ནས། ཞིམ་བུའི་སྐེ་ལ་ག་ཡེར་ཀ་གཡོགས།

Putting a bell on the cat's neck
after the mother of mice was consulted.

*This refers to a story about a wise mother-mouse who, in a wily effort
to help protect her children, tells the cat that the mice wish to award
him a medal for bravery and cleverness. The cat is only too pleased to be
so honored, and so the mice carefully place the award—
a loud, tinkling bell—around the cat's neck. An image of the
immutability of self-interest and the foolishness of vanity.*

རྩིས་པའི་བ་བརླགས། ཨེམ་རྗེའི་མ་གྲོངས།

Even the astrologer's cow gets lost;
even the doctor's mother dies.

There are some things forever beyond even a master's control—
"Time and tide wait for no man."

ཚོང་པས་བསམ་རྒྱ་ཁེ་བཟང་། ཞིམ་བུས་བསམ་རྒྱ་ཙི་ཙི།

A businessman only thinks of profit;
a cat only thinks of mice.

LIKE A YETI CATCHING MARMOTS

ཚིག་རྩུབ་སྨྲ་བའི་གྲོགས་པོ་དེ། ཤ་ཚ་སྙིང་ནས་བྱེད་པའི་དྲགས།

A friend who expresses harsh words loves you from the heart.

Good friends will tell you the truth—
even if the truth sometimes hurts.

མཚོ་ནང་ནས་མཁའི་ཟླ་སྐར་ཀུན། གསལ་ཡང་རང་གི་གཏིང་མི་མཐོང་།

Even though all the reflections of moon and stars appear in the sea, the sea cannot see its own depth.

Even though it is easy to see others' faults and strong qualities, it's difficult to see one's own.

གཞན་གྱི་སྡུག་བསྔལ་སེལ་བ་དེ། དམ་པའི་ཆོས་ཀྱི་སྙིང་པོ་ཡིན།

**Eliminating the suffering of others is
the essence of the sublime Dharma.**

In Buddhism, bodhicitta, *the heartfelt aspiration to save
and serve all other beings, is the most important personal quality
we can cultivate.*

རས་ཞིམ་པོ་ཁྲོ་ཞིངས་ག་ཅིག གཏམ་མི་ཁ་བསྐལ་པ་སྟོང་།

Delicious food lasts for just one meal;
a bad reputation lasts for thousands of eons.

གཟུགས་མེད་གྲིབ་བཙོ་དང་། ཉེས་མེད་ཉེས་འདོགས།

**Creating a shadow without any form,
leveling an accusation without any crime.**

*"Rasing waves where there is no wind"—
an image of manufacturing harmful lies.*

བཟང་པོའི་ལས་ནི་འགྱངས་མི་རུང་། ངན་པའི་གཏམ་ནི་ཤོད་མི་རུང་།

Helpful action shouldn't be put off;
harmful words shouldn't be spoken.

རང་སྲུང་དབང་འདུས། གཞན་སྲུང་ཉེལ་གྱིས་གནོན།

**He who conquers himself,
conquers all.**

རིག་རྩལ་སྤང་ལ་མེ་ཤོར། བཙོན་འགྲུས་རྡོ་ལ་ཨེ་ཁུང་ཕུག

**Cleverness is like a fire ripping through the pasture
and perseverance is like piercing a hole in the rock.**

*Some virtues are flashy and dramatic, like wildfire in a field,
others are slow, subtle, and much harder to see—
like eons of dripping water eroding a hole in a rock—
but just as powerful.
An image encouraging persistent and diligent effort.*

གཡུ་བྱུ་རུ་ཡོད་དུས་སྤོས་ཤེལ་བོར།

Throwing away the amber stone when turquoise and ruby become available.

Leaving an old friend when a new, more impressive or famous one is around.

146

ལག་པ་ལ་ཤ་ཡོད་ན། ནམ་མཁའ་ལ་བྱ་སྡིང་།

Vultures gather when there is meat in one's hand.

And "friends" flock to you when you have something they want.

ལོ་བརྒྱ་སྨན་དང་། འཆི་ཁར་དུག

Medicine for one hundred years and poison at the time of death.

The worldly pleasures that we may spend our life pursuing cannot
save us or comfort us when it comes time to die—
and the more attachment we've cultivated in our lifetime,
the more painful it all is to lose.

ཤ་ཚབའི་ཆེག་དེ་སྦུན་པོ་མེད། ནད་མཐིས་པའི་སྦུན་དེ་ཞིམ་པོ་མེད།

Medicine for jaundice is not sweet;
words spoken out of love are not music to the ear.

Traditional Tibetan medicine can effectively treat the symptoms
of jaundice—but the concoction used to do it is very bitter
and unpleasant to drink.
"Sometimes the truth is a bitter pill to swallow"—
sometimes it's painful to hear what needs to be said.

ཤྭ་བར་ཚ་རིང་ཡང་། གནམ་གྱི་སྐས་ཀ་མི་ཡོང་།

**Even though the antlers of deer are long,
they cannot become ladders to the sky.**

*The use of this proverb is akin to the saying that "When all you have
is a hammer, the whole world looks like a nail." Though a certain
trait may be good to have, it is nonetheless not a panacea.*

ཤིག་གསོད་པར་སྟ་རེ་འཕྱར་མི་དགོས།

There is no need to wield an axe to kill a louse.

An image of overkill—
like trying to use a fire-hose as a water fountain.

ཤིག་དང་འཇེ་བ་སྲོ་མ་གསུམ། ཆེ་སྲོག་དོར་ས་སེན་མོའི་སྐྱེད།

**The flea, louse, and nit each die
under the fingernails.**

*In Tibet, pests like fleas, lice, and nits are killed by being crushed between
the thumbnails—though each is different, the way they die is the same.
Similarly, in the greatest matters of life and death, the differences among
us—our appearance, our job, our relative wealth—
are ultimately of no significance.*

ཤིང་དགྲ་སྟ་རེ་ཡིན་མོད་ཀྱང་། དེ་ཡི་ཡུ་བ་ཤིང་གིས་བྱེད།

**Even though the axe is the tree's natural enemy,
its handle is still made from wood.**

*Sometimes in order to function properly in the world,
we are dependent even upon the existence of our enemies.*

སང་ཉིན་གྱི་ཤ་ལས། དེ་རིང་གི་རུས་པ་ཞིམ།

Today's bone is more delicious than tomorrow's meat.

"A bird in hand is worth two in the bush."

ས་གསར་པ་ལས། འདྲེ་རྙིང་པ་དགའ།

An old demon is better than a new deity.

"It's better to dance with the devil you know than an angel you don't"—
because you never know what's hiding behind an angel's mask.

སྣན་སྐྱེས་ཡོན་ཏན་མེད་གྱུར་ན། ཕྱི་ཆུལ་བཅོས་པས་ཅི་ལ་ཕན།

**If one does not have an inherent quality,
external pretension is of no help.**

*Akin to the opposite meaning of
"Clothes make the man."*

ཨོ་ལོ་དང་གོས་ཆུང་ཆད་ཀྱིན་ཆད་ཀྱིན།

One needs to adjust the clothing to suit to the child.

*In so many of life's situations, there is no
one-size-fits-all solution.*

ཨ་མའི་བུ་ལ་ཡོན་ཏན་ཡོད་ན། དགའ་ལྡན་ཁྲི་ལ་དམ་ཕྲུག་མེད།

**If the mother's son has the necessary qualifications,
the *Gaden* throne is not sealed off to him.**

The Gaden *throne is the highest seat of the Tibetan Gelugpa tradition of
Tibetan Buddhsim—but it's not a hereditary position, so with the right
qualities, anyone of any parentage can in principle occupy it.
Akin to an exhortation to "Aim high, and shoot
for the moon" or the encouragement that
"Where there's a will, there's a way."*

About the Author

PEMA TSEWANG, SHASTRI, a former Fulbright scholar at Harvard University, has served as the chairman of the board of directors for the Tibetan Association of Boston, and has served in various capacities—as principal, headmaster, and teacher of Tibetan language, literature, and history—at schools in the Tibetan Children's Village, and as principal and administrator at the Institute for Buddhist Dialectics Dolmaling, both in Dharamsala, India. He currently works at Wisdom Publications, and has also published many books in Tibetan, including poetry, fiction and nonfiction, and translations of works by Dr. Gene Sharp and Charles Dickens. He lives in Somerville, Massachusetts, with his family.

About Wisdom Publications

WISDOM PUBLICATIONS is dedicated to offering works relating to and inspired by Buddhist traditions. To learn more about us or to explore our other books, please visit our website at www.wisdompubs.org. You can subscribe to our e-newsletter or request our print catalog online, or by writing to:

Wisdom Publications
199 Elm Street
Somerville, Massachusetts 02144 USA
617-776-7416
info@wisdompubs.org

Wisdom is a nonprofit, charitable 501(c)(3) organization and donations in support of our mission are tax deductible.

Wisdom Publications is affiliated with the Foundation for the Preservation of the Mahayana Tradition (FPMT).